SOME VAGUE WIFE

Kathy Lou Schultz

a t e l o s

12

ISBN 1-891190-12-1

First edition, first printing

Acknowledgments:
Grateful acknowledgement is given to the editors of the following publications in which versions of this work first appeared: *Fourteen Hills*, *Lipstick Eleven*, *Narrativity*, *Outlet*, and *Shampoo*.

The image on the cover is a reproduction of "Her Candle Burns Hot" by Susan Bee; it is used with the kind permission of the artist.

ƚ Atelos

A Project of Hip's Road
Editors: Lyn Hejinian and Travis Ortiz
Design: Travis Ortiz
Cover Design: Ree Katrak

SOME VAGUE WIFE

for Robin Tremblay-McGaw and Jim Brashear

Songs

Stories

A Novel

Contents

SONGS

We might have given birth to a butterfly
With the daily news
Printed in blood on its wings

—Mina Loy
Songs to Joannes

The Sonneteer

My essentially receptive positionality reinvented as submission
except for the part that says I liked it

My organs tucked away each morning as a necessary clerkship
complete with starched whites and a pen and clipboard

Invented partnerships result in a heavy schedule
of opera and picnics

Especially because of, or appraised as "a beautiful thing"
though I couldn't decode the appropriate remedy of creams and lotions

There's the pot of paint, the pot of ink, the implements of my derision
or just the daily silver

A number of settings complete with etiquette
when I realized I should have been paying more attention

Now more than ever, in the marriage bed
or when your chickens come home to roost

Memories of you are accompanied by the confusion
of one who knows that the conclusory mechanism is unhinged

Keyless entry systems resulting in all manners of disguise
nonetheless appropriate when I wrap my mouth around it

The daybook reveals minutes spent repasting yesterday's collage
though steam never fails to unloose the resulting total

God, man, don't you know that I meant it and this is no time
to put the spin on pretty baubles

If I seem insistent, this is the final call
and you don't even have a twenty-second timeout

From beyond the arc I've caught a glimpse of you
primping for the camera, tossing your hair off your shoulders

The property-owning class welcomed you with open arms
my cache is fading, I have only this to show for

At one point I wiped the lipstick off the rim
but a flush remained so much as the detritus

of a memory more hardened than the present
by our insistence upon it

It was much this way with us
where sensation replaced flesh, image overrode form

Even now an increase in temperature is possible
despite our facile techniques

I can't say that regret is part of the equation
though we're rushing ferociously toward a equal sign

If I begin by breathing from the diaphragm
the esophageal tendencies are more so

There's a reflex in place where I jerk my hand from the fire
without even having to think about it

The number of seemingly inconsequential incidents colluded
to form first a coincidence, then a pattern

We formed a search party yet the body doesn't reveal any clues
despite the requisite number of openings

Officials on horseback storm the countryside
where we want to believe in a history that can play on the evening news

Connect-the-dots seems a likely map but results in
alphabet soup with crackers

There's nothing so much as a tin can with string
to make me believe you were listening

The advent of streaming media replaces the announcer
with a customizable avatar sporting large breasts

When body parts are interchangeable
each person sees a face in the inanimate

Perhaps this is where I end or decry the present
olfactory humor, unnecessarily negated potential effects

If we only knew the scope of audible knowledge
bound by an experience to believe in

Please let me know when the "x" factor has been defined
or if formulas are still staining the palms with ink

Still a color-coded universe
attempted a justification of your dismissal

If I'm not mistaken there's a bowl of porridge to go with her golden hair
skin the color of an unbaked meringue

By and by the river shall come to you
wading up to the neck

Sadly all cleansing effects are temporary
Looking back, salt our only antecedent

Evening tide sonnet loosed through toothless stem
where a touch waits to bastardize

I traveled the country to search through
a goal as glitter goading me

It's even possible to manufacture purpose
to theorize intent

In the great northeastern corridor
crumbling under the whispered threat of prosperity

The birthplace of democracy
beset by temperaments of weather

Liberty wastes itself on the street corner
folds arms across the chest like armor

No longer content with
breathing through a tube

Belief in a narrative of patriots has now worn thin
but books are still worth their weight

I've placed a bet that may or may not pay off
but for now I'm in the game

There's only the possibility of forward motion
to begin the day

Feminized intent to gather the luscious
hunger and sweet and salt

I press him into and upon me
memorizing points of pressure, of rhythm

That call to other plains I've visited
eager to return

Only this daily, though, this weather
the air fueling seasons for passing

Quickly I press a narrative into service
to substitute for the leaky center

Now in the Mid-Atlantic southern flavors
the itch you cannot scratch

Or girlhood a thing I've parlayed for cash
a kind of uneven barter that justifies my existence

Even past hoping for hope or wanting for want
implosion the next order of business

Where lust is altogether unbecoming
take cover from hunger

I imagine a "you" to meet the "me"
that keeps flapping its gums

Under and over, and in between
passing static across time zones

Finally, as if always, on top of
aims to please her, pleasure, ridden or wrested from
by the time of her confession, confusion
unknown destination, lack of reason
plagued with expectation
frayed or frightened, for her justification.

What I mean is I didn't plan it
though I can't let go of it
intention my religion by this time heretical
while you breathe beside me
no way of knowing it, showing it
forestalling it, recalling it
justification replaces all of it,
my hand resting on your heart.

That New Exile

A Sonnet after "The Wife's Lament" for Emily Steiner

I can say I have not suffered
But we should live far from words
At dawn I set out then to search deep waves
Laid in secret, tossing with longings
Part old world, each wide wanderer that man's kinsmen
Forsook so that as now I am most wretchedly up

I was where my sorrow grew such hardships
These from my family I draw in or
By the anguish of this world
Since his lord might be fretted to us first
To her plans
A lot my sorrow for the I, for the other
My lord, my man, tortured, friendless, seized in the
sadness that new exile

STORIES

What is the use of a violent kind of delightfulness
if there is no pleasure in not getting tired of it.

—Gertrude Stein
Tender Buttons

Order of Law

There just isn't enough energy for it all. Like not being able to run the toaster oven and the microwave at the same time. It's not what you expect. Or seldom is. Like at age 31, realizing that the bourgeois nuclear family is my only protection from the bourgeois nuclear family.

My mistake with the last one was falling in love. It makes me feel tragic — or rabid. His father was more my type: surly in a way that meant something.

These days I carry a copy of Industrial Welfare Commission Order No. 4-98 in my bag as insurance: See, I have documentation. The Law.

Who believes they have rights? It's not a rhetorical question.

My friend believes in Marx the way my brother believes in God. Kathy Acker's death shocking, a warning for what I must prepare against. And then the story about the Literary Executor for the Literary Executor (not Kathy's) and how they all had AIDS. Contingencies.

And still I wanted to believe in the clear choice: the right one and the wrong one and the possibility of finding the former.

No combination of good and bad satisfied me.

He says you put out a lot of feminine energy, and instead I hear "you put out a lot."

He says I have a pretty face, and I think "are you calling me fat?"

He says a pretty face is important. He says a pretty flies in the face. Putting your best face forward. Face to face. A license to carry mace.

I wake up on my 31st birthday and don't want to get out of bed. I've lost track of the reasons and what little sense. Rhymes with fence. Is the door to your attraction open? *Yes, I find it to be open. I could possibly be attracted, er. . . distracted. Certainly impacted.*

What's the secret to getting out of bed? Keeping your head. A ground wire that allows me to fly wildly over thc edge.

I dreamt about Frank Sinatra. A young Sinatra in super-hip suit jackets and shoes. Then I dreamt I was a whore.

In tender moments he called me his Sweet Slut. Something about him allowed me to be fully possessed, my sexuality open.

All the men at the party over thirty were married. We said

the guy in the leather pants could carry it off if he were European — maybe.

I fussed around the edges of an old wound. Couldn't keep my hands off it, the hole growing wider. Cutting valentine hearts from red construction paper, trimming them toward perfection over and over until there's nothing left.

Or simply that it's me and not other. Even if it is.

Dodie turns up the "D" in degenerate. The irony that fucking boys — not girls — made me into a first-class pervert. I laid claim to his dick like it was my own — a rightful part of myself gone missing. This one said he couldn't fuck me without getting emotionally involved. He could clasp both of my wrists in one muscled hand. Prone, I lay on top of him, my body floating on an island.

In a semi-trance state he discovers his desire to kill his mother. He says, "Many women had paid for what you have done." In fairy tales, Mom is always to blame. My left thumbnail refuses to adhere. If I were to fall in love, I'd have to bring the white trash with me. I hide my guilty desire to spend long periods of time alone.

Of course, when I wanted something, I always knew it. The very intensity of my desire keeping it out of reach (or so I believed). She kept herself from fear or disappointment by turning off her own desire completely — while I was filled voraciously with need. Greed, while unbecoming in a woman, is prized in men.

Another claimed that my very presence increased his need to be more "manly." He opened doors for me, refused cute pet names, and fucked me righteously.

My body demanded something to show for itself. Writing is thievery, as in stealing time.

Anxiety is a sticky substance infused with fear. Dollar for dollar. Or, for instance, poverty. My own collusion in bourgeois appearances bleeding me dry. The need to be seen or recognized outweighing other emotional vaunts. Every song he laid in my ear keeping my mouth and nose above water.

But respiration takes place in lack of desire. Once your head hits the floor, the body resumes intake and expiration. The old in and out.

Anger, not sex, is what makes a girl really bad.

My Very Silly Gender Story

for / after Elizabeth Treadwell

Dear Elizabeth,

Can I be your biggest fan? If I were, I would be called a groupie, because we commonly come in groups.

Unlike lesbians, who come in bunches — like bananas.

One day it occurred to me: I didn't have to marry a rock star, I could BE a rock star. (Insert desired profession or quality here ____ .) For Hilary it didn't work out so good; she still had to marry the president.

When I was a girl, I fucked a boy in the ass. And afterward, I was still a girl.

When I wore lipstick people smiled at me more and were pleased.

Public Transport

Rasta man   lifts his son up
Maw of bulldozer chews the earth   "did you see?"
Little boy eyes gleam   brown and green
The face of nations   turns
Waves   "bye-bye"

Story

Prologue

He is deterred by openings, by blood in the sky, by black on white. Fear buzzing along my nerves, its own soliloquy. The low drone of your denial underneath in counterpoint. Body slows to the pace of swallows. Smoke roaring from the fire signals the exact moment when it's too late. Weather a contraption brought in from another country. My refusals meant nothing, my body jangling along as if desire constituted a map.

1

In the next chapter I kept repeating myself as if construction meant memory. It was all something I'd reconstituted with the available water left from the quake. The agency set up for preparedness arrived late, having not received the memo. They complained bitterly and donned paper hats, surrounding a white car. I had no excuse so I slipped from the crowd and made my way toward the fire brightening the sky.

2

There was no getting over which animal was the dumbest. By this time, we were down to crumbs. You wanted to lick between my fingers, but I wrapped the silver blanket around me more tightly. You showed me a picture to remind me what you look like, but I pointed out it was obvious you'd torn it from a magazine: just look at the jagged edges.

3

Others believed your obvious hijinx and I was left to roll my eyes and pout. You leaned in and whispered, "You don't wear it well," and I swatted you away with the increasing number of flies. Officials who couldn't make it onto the helicopter fled on foot while we waved, listlessly.

4

A woman in a puffy pink coat grabbed my arm but this was after I had woken up. Your voice clogged my throat like bits of dust. You complained that I kept you awake and I said no one asked you here. We expected a convoy any minute, but they had lost our address.

5

I kept mistaking your hand in my pocket for my own and startled in fright when I couldn't feel my fingers. This became a kind of theatre where you're expecting a dinner that never arrives. Your mother would have known a way out of this, but she kept refusing my calls.

6

Had we a television, we would have seen ourselves on the screen wearing mismatching plaids. In remote parts of the country, this was mistaken for the latest in urban fashion. I couldn't shut my mouth for the life of me, so I concentrated on yours. Later it was revealed that the transfusion had been incomplete because of a kink in the hose.

7

After this I lost my appetite, and stood in front of the open cupboards staring at the dusty boxes and cans. A letter had arrived directing you to the next port. You tried to hide it in your shoe, but I noticed your awkward limp. The wrestling that ensued raised a cloud of dust that aggravated our asthma. This reminded us to return to our separate corners as if a bell had rung.

8

I was gallant and helped you pack your bag. When I had carried it to the curb, you rushed forward with a determinacy that suggested "goodbye" severs the splice in the film. The tape whipped wildly through the air threatening to sever the heads of the growing number of onlookers. I recognized them from the previous calamity and asked them to kindly step aside.

9

It was clear that a genetic accident was hurtling us toward a sequel in which I played a secretary about to receive a job with a pension. You would have never stood for this, so I covered the doors and windows anticipating your return. When the ending resulted in nothing more than popcorn, the audience rushed the screen and tried to rip it from the wall. I recognized you in the red beard you wore as a disguise. You should have tried, instead, to conceal the shape of your head.

10

I went underground communicating with you through the copper pipes. The banging that ensued roused mice from their holes alerting the city fathers who burst from behind closed doors adjusting their suspenders and wiping spittle from the corners of the mouths. When confronted with this knowledge, I would later say that I had been asleep or out walking the dog. On the 14th of each month, citizens in remote areas still raise a flag in your honor, thinking you a hero.

Animal Primer
(a horror story)

CAT
If I alter the climate with my spray can, line up to ingest false estrogens. Nonetheless a restless tick that results in reproduction. Here, kitty, kitty. A doll with your face is much more practical than a child who requires 17 years of education. If I was somebody's mama, then who would I be?

BIRD
And now, the fear that pesticides are being absorbed through my feet and entering the bloodstream, that a fruit salad is an industrial accident waiting to happen. But I just want to get my whites whiter. At the picnic I fell asleep in the sun, and there came a time when my nails curled around my toes like a falcon's.

INSECT
Add Lyme disease to the list. And my people were not designed for this climate. Just stop growing lawns in Arizona; it's the desert.

GIRAFFE
Twisting about on my neck like a balloon, like an unexpected lodestar. All the better to reach the higher, more succulent leaf. It's human nature to construct faces everywhere, to make shapes of clouds. Please duck, clearance is only 6'1".

ZEBRA
Spots make me blend in with the fauna, but here there's only 1 1/2 white people. Please check yourself and report to the front. Gas mask optional.

BOA CONSTRICTOR
The log across my chest is only your arm, but this doesn't make breathing any easier. Please avoid the neck; it's where I keep my throat. If I put my finger in your ear the sounds emanating from your head indicate signs of life.

A NOVEL

Fiction must stick to the facts, and the truer the facts the better the fiction—so we are told.

—Virginia Woolf
A Room of One's Own

Some Vague Wife

Thought is without comparison to the body what the body is to the speed of light for the letter
—Nicole Brossard

1

Prologue

Realized with a start that in his real life. When I was younger I would. Faced the beach. Had the unaccountable sensation that. Enchanted by the hundred or so silvery white locks. Eagerly took the train. Had had a recurring dream. I know it would be worse for me if. Also he never laughs.

As if I had been given permission. Lulled by the last fierce heat. There was a line you crossed. A very young, barefoot, willful-looking woman wearing a long dark dress. Some of the euphoria I once felt. Like the mouths of fish. Also, there were pictures of women.

They never stopped at the appointed hour. I'm talking serious stiletto. Which was as insistent as a brass door knocker. They called them "Big Women." I feel like I haven't breathed in three weeks.

Your voice doesn't scratch my itch. Through the white clothing I'd brought with me. In a kind of learned officiousness that struck me as unnatural. Writing skits about the proper behavior of workers.

An unrehearsed emotional subjectivity. The transgressive desire. Have never been good at accepting that I cannot have what I want. And so I have lived. I have lived against that which is a refusal. The body's final subjugation.

To traverse an emotional distance across the bodies buried there. Impossible to separate reality from history — the mythologic artifact of existence. Always writing in a story, another story, which constructs what we believe has happened, though no two people can agree. Mouth to mouth, divulging secrets of the other order.

There's something about writers. They're damned hard to re-educate. My father was pitiless in depicting his own failures. I couldn't find my way out, and the guards were as unhelpful as any other Parisian.

Fashion excited them. His face was horribly contorted. When asked by an adult to give an accounting of himself. Or someone she barely knew for example. On hands and knees. And discover that Athena was a flunky of the male order that had created her.

I didn't see why she hadn't split. And other men's wives at random. I washed my hands real good and greased them. That making love with her caused this sad, pitiful behavior. He said the blood from the slaughterhouse stayed under his nails.

I have consulted no one, out of loyalty to her. Marvelled at and admired by all of us. Only this dogged attempt to finish something. A man of men. Whimsical, maybe just plain crazy.

Down the short ramp grilled like a cage. If he is found a lunatic or becomes of unsound mind. Is especially struck with the number of false starts, the hesitancy, the backtracking.

By opposite paths. Is plunged. The faintest idea of being there. His hands on my face.

The day is a nightmare unless you work. Staring out the waist-high windows. Exasperated laugh at how they have complicated everything. Time to get my luggage and go.

All I can tell you is that he was familiar, comfortable; and what's more emotionally recognizable. A scar, a map I burned through. Charging from place to place as if a direction. The wanting and the impossible task of identifying the object.

The source of my ruin. Brain, vowel of fog. Lithe and nearly crushed beneath my chest.

All distance was perceived as rupture and therefore persecuting. A hallucination which begins with a sunset and ends with blood on the walls.

Not a notice. Decisions arrive by mail, irrefutable. Up against my inscrutable origins. Particularly if my behavior is faultless. Though not taken as title.

If granted a degree. Pressure point, wrist, a throat left open. She is still asking herself where this body — her body — ought to be, where exactly to put it, so that it will cease to be a burden to her.

She is erecting a scaffolding which is temporarily necessary for her, a woods, a field of wheat, patience. To stabilize her image by constantly inspecting it. The old mimetic mirror?

Some of the youngest and prettiest members. With a perfume she had made that smelled amazingly like fresh water. Proved something that he felt needed proving. And being legally married seconded that opinion.

You mean the body. That fucking him was no longer a possibility, but an inevitability. Wearing platform shoes. The excitement in her approach to me now. Not a feminist foot soldier. You are incommunicado here then.

Very particular hell over this. Just so I could see her face again. Adoring lust before this amazement. And then the door slams shut.

Wearing his gender uneasily. In the air just now. A courting man. Tired man from the dead.

They will kill him with money and credit. Creatures not even separate or at odds, but subject. Feeling that in all important respects it was already over. Here's a statement false or true: "Have never been able to accept that I can have what[ever] I want." Inside my textuality. Turning him over and over.

It's not the woman we were promised. With a vague prognosis that I might just return to normality. Her elegance, both when she moved and when she was in repose, was upsetting. Looking for or discovering something. Completely undone.

The tall, thin body of the other woman would have appeared little by little. A crush of women waiting for the bus. She devours them with her eyes; she invents them.

Strewn. Where the quarrel magically resumes as an interior dialogue. Or "after" meaning as when a psychotic no longer uses words to signify.

She keeps advancing toward me at the same pace. Prepared to get to her feet if anyone makes a move. Adding up the costs in meticulous fashion.

(Lemon, late afternoon light. Lawn of torso.)

The dress and its panties. An interval between the morning and the evening. After a stint in the care and feeding of others.

I slit open each envelope. I replaced the gun in its holster. I read the schedule for departures and arrivals. I separated each page from its likeness.

A poverty of speech. To bed me down. To misperceive and yet lucidity. No food from age fourteen. What it all meant. Inside the body as in a shadowbox of clues.

Monitored the comings and goings and the equality of exchange. With one foot planted firmly in the mouth.

He would have divested her slowly of her black dress, and by the time he had done it, a good part of the voyage would have been over. Distilled frame by frame.

Not interested in the possible implications for semiotics. With some modifications to the neckline.

I am a woman and a soldier. I mean I drive a bus between unspecified locations. I mean as a child. Dressed in drag at the fifties dance and wondered why all the women wanted to dance with her.

You were here. You were not. Here. I mean there. I mean inside.

Pale. Pallid. Paint. Red paint. Stained. The lips. The lips stained red.

After years of taking in how a woman should be, what a desirable woman should look like, she began to feel that she was becoming one and was therefore acceptable.

"Usurper" of masculine perogative. Gender fuck as good as any. Exchanged them on the train. Impossible to rediscover by mail.

Relentlessly personal. Not hammered at, but slipping in sideways. The last digit. As if in relief.

2

A Warm Calamity

The sissy persists as a comedic object. Turning over tables of mom's bone china. All the better to butter my toast. When he pulls my hand into his lap. Good phone being a quality I admire in a girl when I open my throat and beg.

Despite my obvious disbelief in your hyper-constructed textual real. Here's my advice to you: stop relying on your old heterosexual acrobatics. Stunts which outstrip demand.

Although at first blush the tunes may seem similar, they are in fact not the same song. Acerbic counterpoint to the opening and shutting of her mouth. The visual equivalent to unexamined foreplay.

Praise poised tongues dusted off for reuse. He sucks his breath in, eyes shut tightly. Hips slip to fake. Pick and roll where the ball toss eludes his roving eye's inconsistent trajectory. Lackadaisical lips reform pretty overtures.

Teeth release what's caught under the skin. A body worn loosely. A system of leverages to incorporate distribution of weights. I pry the leather strap from his hand as in the smallest gesture he brushes the hair from my face and I board the train.

Now there was nothing between him and "it," as he called what he currently felt. His arms wrapped loosely around that particular leg.

Knife pleats box malignant gestures. The passengers assumed a distinct anonymity, despite the need to stand hip to hip, thigh to thigh. The need to stay on schedule drove the workmen to distraction, like laying out a project an inch off in step one.

The sleeping bodies arrange themselves. A series of breaks and pleasures. Familiarity breeds. I was his first homosexual relationship: the one he needed before he could move on to other women.

A cabin, where I was born in the 60s, a long time before. Regions known respectively as the Plains, the Badlands, and the myths and legends surrounding.

I drop into an older writer's unpublished manuscript: a new character in a scene which has already happened. I turn to fucking as a religion; the only thing which hasn't happened, the dick I have yet to suck.

My wanting opens doors to other forms of desire, when

I lie wide open, phone in hand mechanically clicking off digits. Your gender is a skin I wear then put away after tiring. My skin's much too rosy, I'm pink through and through.

Sometimes I want to leave evidence, like the woman with a bright red lipstick neatly stroking, "Thanks for blocking the driveway" on a car's windshield.

Wonder Woman herself sometimes got trapped in this either/or choice. As she muses to herself: "Some girls love to have a man stronger than they are to make them do things. Do I like it? I don't know, it's sort of thrilling. But isn't it more fun to make a man obey?"

Avoid interiority despised by playwrights putting words in the mouths of dolls. Grinning figures scrubbed free of prior evidence. I paint your mouth for you. I check your teeth for breaks and fissures, rubbing each surface with my index finger. Open wide, I mean, relax and take it.

Kissing him was a habit, something to close the spaces between feeling alive.

Sex as ritualistic as my attempt to enter you unnoticed, following the flight pattern of certain migratory birds. Your movements betray past affairs, stuttering speech effects drawn from low-impact encounters. Cravings leave a sharp, burning taste like your mouth after whiskey.

It's not this movie we're in; during your last double-take I've turned the tables ever so slightly that you've lost your place among my bodily furniture. It's my mind you haven't kept up with, unknowingly drawing conclusions and novelist endings. My acrobatic melodramas take place alone, moving you at the speed of my machinations.

My body is not a destination. I move through it at the slightest suggestion of sentiment. Between his body and the door, midnight and 5 a.m., orgasm sweeps up.

Surly girl story results in knowing glances. The smallest gesture — leaning in to brush the hair from her face.

My sudden adornment reveals my disagreement with ancient codes of proliferation and need. Stampeding effects which march you right back where you came from, missy. These lips are mere appositions to another form of devouring.

A girl for every pocket. Pretty plastic feet adorn rigid mass-produced ankles.

On this day, my intentionality was revealed, and really, was it so bad after all? I spotted you a mile away and took action described as "cunning." Vertiginous female desire, and you complied so nicely, knee socks pulled up and hands folded in your lap. White is your color, but I knew better. Later we would say we felt

21 again, though he had insomnia and agitated me with his exhaustion.

Proximity produces the static electricity of dreams like changes in your barometric pressure. The only medium of exchange centimeters of blood drawn haphazardly across white space, the gap created when you press your chest against mine.

Mainly you're hovering somewhere above or behind me, connected in our tenacity to avoid possession. Little girls call you in the middle of the night, and you follow after, caught in a fugue of overgrown wish fulfillment. The play button on your remote is broken, but my lips move of their own accord.

When the boundaries collapsed, there was nothing left to feed on but ourselves. My anger a fragile screen against which I could feel my heels pressing. She was ground for me. A smooth, round surface revolving.

My aloneness now requires that I measure thought, break down the long strings that take up their own momentum. Ropey distractions which elude my fingertips.

Now there's no telling which of us makes the next move. My toe's on the line waiting to dart out, shave off that last second. The starter's pistol looks tinny and childlike, creating too much of a glare in the sun.

3

For A Married Man Springing Powers

A gift for the hyperbolic ensures that the quest for satiation continues even after fucking when I turn away and he places his hand on my shoulder. The announcement of the inconsistency of his attraction a screen through which emotionality settles into a gritty sediment. At night I grind my teeth down to small nubs, milk teeth which take the wince out of my bite.

He was clever. He had an arch, subtle voice that he used to good effect as an instrument of his cleverness. A slow pursuit of winks and nods. Televised breaks in your own attention span allow me to settle the body more firmly.

Linguistic latitudes pry open perception's restive slumber. The final walk-out an insight into the boredom created by ingrown tropes, misspent passions littered about five decades of rooms.

With a carnation in his buttonhole coming towards him. As if there rolled down to him, vigorous, unending, his future.

Despite the echo of his footsteps behind me. Mistakes

him for a housebreaker. No talent for the group mind of criminality, a vertigo which overtakes him when confronted with the presence of others.

This prairie town still has a downtown cut through with a main street inlaid with individual bricks. Modern suburbia mocks this effect with piousness, slick replications of backdrop and emotion. Your disgruntlement can't change originality or even your own attempt to corner the market. Ritual of commodification and fetishes of the heart. An orgasm of my own design.

Suddenly we're up to our necks, testing the other's ability to swim. A sibling rivalry marked by your incestuous glances. A stern hand on the crown of my head pushing me under. I break the surface. I pause to consider. I produce syllables of ingratiating acceptance beneath an insoluble blackness, an oily tension I crack with the forcibility of laughter.

The turbulence of your touch produced anxiety similar to the fickleness of weather. With her angular grim smile. Fresh as if issued to children on a beach.

A touch of the bird about her. Was going that very night to kindle and illuminate. Then the hour, irrevocable.

Time supplants the perfectly upholstered body. The distance between two aesthetics excuses and evades. Sliding, just then, almost imperceptibly, his hand up my skirt.

The locus of fertility now hard to locate, much as who pays the check and what this means, if anything, later in bed, and who remembers and so on.

If the world of objects remains stopped, caught in my livid expression to uncover connectivity, then the world of signs must at least be at the next train station. You recall that the fare, being one-way, must be repaid in the exact gesture before returning.

In light of little boys' well-known fascination with motor vehicles, we might call this tendency to *vroom vroom vroom* their way through rapprochement.

And then this business of taking out a stick of rouge, or a powder puff and making up in public.

Since she was lying on the sofa, cloistered, exempt, the presence of this thing which she felt to be so obvious became physically existent.

A viable sexual arithmetic supplants the lexical semaphore. No amount of backpedaling to close the physical distance created by rabid, I mean rampant, ambivalence. The required girl depicted in an instructional video for home use.

My tongue traces the plane of your neck beginning with

the small indentation beneath your left ear lobe. Tasting trajectories bound by hyperbolic emotionality. Gently probing your girl-soft skin.

Go, big, gift. Beat, nosebleed, evenly, easy. Now, out, loud.

Blood to flatter the other father. Deeply deviant plastic strategies. Spare to utter the venal narcissist. Quell a step toward symbiotic seduction.

Form to hold harmless otherwise evade. Trap splatters aperture protrusion. Nearing cleave divisive holding. Slippery staircase, slope to heart.

4

Toward Fissures Forming Plots

Time splits an axis. No edification to revise my inviting you in. Solid hands and forearms. A subtle hemorrhage across a hemisphere of grief. Obliterated pain mechanics. Lingering vestigial electricity, memory of your shuddering body.

Explosive domestic paralysis. My neck, my breast, heel it. Bitter, unrestrained fugue. Toe box, this torpid distance. All my girlstuff real and bruisy. Swelling octagonal aperture. A hiccup or sneeze dream, baby.

Characters tend toward fissures forming plots as expected as his handprint on my ass. Body as named other. Cervix and helix. Milk-heavy.

Paperwhites. Stiff-lipped. Tongues pass through this delicate chamber. Or what passes for ourselves. The careening of desires, toppling.

Here in the earliest social interaction we see how the search for recognition can become a power struggle: how assertion becomes aggression.

The ideology of opposites falsely proposed masculine and feminine as two halves of a whole, when I knew them to be costume — drag and accompanying accoutrements. With the knowledge that a shorter skirt got me a better seat on the bus, I bared my lipstick and faced the world. Now we're driving in circles; though faced with an eerie deja vu, the tour continues in a neverending loop of mathematical infinity.

Heavy with desire. Blue-lidded. A little strut remakes my machine, folded into my brown-eyed boy.

Prone to sentimental excess. My face reseen as blank page. Casting about for his own image to reflect. "Two immigrants from that beautiful other place."

She had always, even as a girl, a sort of timidity, which in middle age becomes conventionality, and then it's up, it's all up he thought, looking rather drearily into the glassy depths, and wondering whether by calling at that hour he had annoyed her; overcome with shame suddenly at having been a fool; wept; been emotional; told her everything, as usual, as usual.

His wife was crying, and he felt nothing; only each time she sobbed in this profound, this silent, this hopeless way, he descended another step into the pit.

Our bodies expand, contract along lines of comfort or

unease. Splaying myself open, then, your face forming itself in front of me, slowly as if unseen. Dismantled, the excitement, the gravity, unplanned kisses made me real.

If you will come

I shall put out
new pillows for
you to rest on

Super-sensory abstinence. Your leaving cleaves my visible heart. Uncustomarily good-bye, the electronic pinpoints converge into no whole. Just these fits of memory startled by severity.

You may forget but

Let me tell you
this: someone in
some future time
will think of us

Guilt by association of need. Epistemology of bloodlessness. Another finger in and he relaxes. My pronouns slip inside my shiny purse.

Lips as full as, your slippery touch. All day desire radiates through this house of my own making.

5

Adjustable Perches

My boy-girl princess all groovy this evening, sharp with elbows and shoulder blades. Desire across boundaries too sharp to cross. 24 hours of comfortable heat.

Our skins slide across. Sweet-cheeked girl peck. A baby's unformed milky bones.

A pact to reflect daily resonances. "I miss you," means "Do you miss me?"

A cupboard and a roof. Rough wooden shelves soaked with white paint. The smell of oil flares our nostrils.

Your hand encloses mine, ratifying physical laws when you dismantle me step by step. My weeping fresh and startling, you contract your awe-struck mouth. Anticipatory like the smell of rain.

The temptation to bring you inside, where the light slants across my desk, warming my pale skin. Afternoon lassitude of linguistic junk. White boats across the lake.

Returning is a grand gesture emphasizing departure. When I finally lose sight of you, the earth still suspends my body in its animation.

My freshly parted hair still damp from the morning, when you turned, wanting me, all sleepy-eyed softness.

The road ahead craggy and distant multiples our longing, my breath in hiccups, false stops until we find the wave that continues.

We proceed as if finding bread crumbs on a trail.

The containment I experience through your matter-of-fact nod proceeds outbursts designed to unloose your fibrillar emotions. Dichotomies which bore me.

What's the gift, the partial barter, which promotes our stasis — you waiting for disintegration, and I for a stable distance. I can accept your intimacy in your absence.

Words an elevated foreground, everywhere falling fictive, furious scatter shot. I slip the pellet underneath my tongue, hidden in an enclosure of human temperature.

In our shared understanding, there are few formulas to interpret this new-found wound, wound round characters you describe as real. Goals program the future requiring the abstraction of my body in front of you.

Time telescopes individual events, cheating clarity. Metaphysical photos, faces sunk in relief. For now, kiss me in the way I remember and let us look into the light of the morning.

6

Epilogue

Her indestructible thighs. A vertical line going south. From belly button to pubic bone. Brand-new scar.

She wears high heels like in dreams. Stunned. Apostate.

I could have said he only fell for tragic women, but I was falling for tragic men. You know, their darkness, their pain. "You light up my life, you give me hope, to carry on," Debby Boone was singing to *me*.

I turned to my girlfriends. They had strong shoulders and clear thoughts. Wedged in the back seat, her arm brushed against my breast and rested there.

A man who saw the world through film, but experienced a lack of vision. A man I encounter through dailiness, through habit. A man with the hands of my father.

Distance spreads. Across your lips.

Your hips move me. Hand in glove.

Pink. Drawn into the skin. All summer. Or all winter. Scripted. Cut.

Rushing headlong in with the body and checking positions later. Velocity.

Or when his dreadlocks were a lot less polite looking. That it was all fair game. Down to the very last vowel. Avowal.

Two loulous wrapped rapt in bed sheets.

Baby's got Mingus Fingers. All around and through me. To thrill me.

Baby done gone and you know it know. Something to show for. Here and before now. Baby done proved it.

All in a groove now. Here and before now. Oh, baby, you knew it.

Girl to girlness reveals a surety surfeit. Our beliefs clamoring for real estate.

Churl. Countryman. Highlander.

Every possible apology or minimization. Privation. Dilation.

She dressed with her back to him, then left the motel room and walked down to the water. Bare-legged and bare-armed in her cotton jersey dress.

She had a sense that the dream had ended and she had slept on. Further and farther. Up and away.

The first time he entered me he said, "I think we've got a match baby," and I sealed this sentence in my heart and swallowed the key.

Unmatched by, "I think I'm falling in love with you, you son-of-a-bitch," and later this made me smile, laughing at myself.

What she was staving off or holding out against. A grammar of indeterminancy. A cold water walk-up.

She had watched them in supermarkets and knew the signs. All the indices of the idle lonely.

Happiness came like an unmarked box without directions. She kept trying to catch herself in it, afraid it would pass without her noticing.

Inscribing my language upon him. Brush strokes along the abdomen. Purple-black nipples. Smooth, round ass.

Endless expanse of what if. Figure brought into fruition. A thorough dressing down. Round or through me. A voice on the wire.

Or if I wrote "wife." Rife. Theocracy. Meritorious.

Mercy. For the woman's clandestine, zippered heart. Miles I have come before you. Previously unknown.

Everyone got what he came for. A schedule to rival the master's. Departures and arrivals. A vagabond. A conductor.

Miles I crossed the desert for water. Previously alone.

At the end of it all a ringing phone and she does not rise to answer it. It twitters at the edges of her sleep.

Verboten. Far gone.

She wonders if this will be one of those evenings when something unimaginable would occur. And the language used to describe it later.

What he was willing to do for her, and the sexiness of that. Eroticization of her pleasure.

He covers the receiver with his palm and turns away.

I arranged everything and at the appointed hour the three of them arrived. Before any words were spoken, I recognized him by the sound of his breathing.

She drove her new BMW up to the GoodWill and was confused by the people staring. I smiled and tried to act "natural."

I was the second man to fuck him. The first he met while he was still in school. "Don't you go to UCLA?" It was a kind of code.

At the end of the day, his body a destination. Miles on a train I have traveled postponing pleasure. Our voices hang in the air, I touch myself.

Miles I have traveled to hear his breathing. Loudly overtaking him in sleep, a comforting wheeze which lulls me.

Prone. His locks falling forward across his face. My dick gets hard just looking at his ass.

There can be no question or assumption. The girlfriend in L.A. The fits of rage or depression. The unshakable self-centeredness. All waiting to be read like a dime store novel.

My narrative spins out like a car in the rain.

Our lives a careening that could have taken us anywhere. The sheer random force of it underscoring her belief.

She weaves a web of talk. Contentment, stranger to this snare.

Used to desire, but uncomfortable with need. She covers her head with the blanket to keep from shivering.

The whiteness of my arms practically glowing in the dimmed light, up against his dark, supple skin.

When I fucked him, a high, clear-pitched sigh rang out from his mouth each time he exhaled. "Go easy, baby," he said. And I withdrew my dick, softly, gently exploring his ass until I gave it to him once again harder. He tossed his head back sharply, his locks raining off his face.

Fists of wanting. Emboldened by grief. A world apart. Of frost.

No sooner than. No later. Had she walked to the door. Bereft.

Solidity in solitude. A place in the life cycle. Searching on hands and knees.

He fucked me so hard that I bled. Four fingers in my cunt, nearly a fist.

"What I feel for you now is all I will ever feel for you." And ever. A straightjacket.

Given to histrionics. Or expected.

Protected more than risked.

Stutter. Choke. Recede.

My arms a fortress.

Each flag in a field.

The harder my dick, the wetter his pussy. The deeper I fucked him, the more open he became.

Atelos was founded in 1995 as a project of Hip's Road and is devoted to publishing, under the sign of poetry, writing that challenges the conventional definitions of poetry, since such definitions have tended to isolate poetry from intellectual life, arrest its development, and curtail its impact.

All the works published as part of the Atelos project are commissioned specifically for it, and each is involved in some way with crossing traditional genre boundaries, including, for example, those that would separate theory from practice, poetry from prose, essay from drama, the visual image from the verbal, the literary from the non-literary, and so forth.

The Atelos project when complete will consist of 50 volumes.

The project directors and editors are Lyn Hejinian and Travis Ortiz. The director for text production and design is Travis Ortiz; the director for cover production and design is Ree Katrak.

Atelos (current volumes):

1. *The Literal World*, by Jean Day
2. *Bad History*, by Barrett Watten
3. *True*, by Rae Armantrout
4. *Pamela: A Novel*, by Pamela Lu
5. *Cable Factory 20*, by Lytle Shaw
6. *R-hu*, by Leslie Scalapino
7. *Verisimilitude*, by Hung Q. Tu
8. *Alien Tatters*, by Clark Coolidge
9. *Forthcoming*, by Jalal Toufic
10. *Gardener of Stars*, by Carla Harryman
11. *lighthouse*, by M. Mara-Ann
12. *Some Vague Wife*, by Kathy Lou Schultz

Distributed by:

Small Press Distribution
1341 Seventh Street
Berkeley, California
94710-1403

Atelos
P O Box 5814
Berkeley, California
94705-0814

to order from SPD call 510-524-1668 or toll-free 800-869-7553
fax orders to: 510-524-0852
order via e-mail at: orders@spdbooks.org
order online from: www.spdbooks.org

Some Vague Wife
was printed in an edition of 1,000 copies
at Thomson-Shore, Inc.
The cover was printed at Southeastern Printing.
Text design and typesetting by Lyn Hejinian and Travis Ortiz
using the Adobe version of the classic typeface
Garamond for the text and Cheltenham for the titles.
Cover design by Ree Katrak.